The Seller's Grail

A Little Book with BIG Results to Help You Sell Your Home Quick!

By Julie Wyrick

Selling your home may be stressful and nerve wracking. Most sellers do not even know where to begin. With this book I hope to ease that burden for you. I have compiled a list of tips and tricks to help you sell your home quick! This book will give you ideas on everything from how to prepare yourself mentally and your home physically. I hope you enjoy!

About Me

For a quick introduction my name is Julie Wyrick. I am a graduate of the University of Alabama at Birmingham with a degree in Cytotechnology. I worked at a lab for over 10 years as a Cytotechnologist while doing professional photography on the side. I discovered my love for real estate when I started taking pictures of homes for local listings. I quickly learned that I enjoy working with people and helping them sell their homes fast. So, I ended my career as a Cytotechnologist and joined a real estate investment firm. I learned the ins and outs of successfully selling a home and doing it with ease.

I am now a licensed real estate agent and enjoy the grind of a fast-paced career. I have been coached by some of the best real estate professionals in the industry and I hope to share some of this knowledge with you. I wrote this book to help people, like yourself, sell their home and do it in record time!

Introduction

This book is intended to simplify the process of selling your home. It will give you tips on what to do before listing your home and tell you what to expect while your home is on the market. Each section is intended to educate the seller, because putting your home on the market doesn't have to be a daunting task.

Table of Contents

Declutter	12
Clean Your Home	14
Personal Items	16
Pets	17
Staging	18
Valuables	19
Curb Appeal	21
Real Estate Agent	23
For Sale by Owner	26
Pictures	27
3D Tours/ Drone Aerial Shots	30
Lighting	32

Smells 34

Upgrades 35

Set Your Home Apart 37

Timing 38

Tough Skin 40

Advertising 42

Open House 44

Ask for Feedback 46

Home Health Inspection 47

Loan Programs 49

Closing Costs 50

Pricing 51

My Wish for You 53

Declutter

Before you put your home on the market, you may want to consider decluttering your life. Especially if you have extra items laying around that aren't needed for every day living. Consider getting a portable storage unit temporarily. Non-every day life items can be stored in the unit, this will allow less clutter in the house. Do not store and stack everything into your closets. Buyers tend to want to see how much storage or closet space a property has. If they view your closets and they are filled with extra "stuff", they may think your home is lacking in space and may turn them off from your property. You should only need that storage until for a small amount of time, because your goal is to sell your home *FAST*! Then once your house sells that portable storage unit can be delivered to your new residence.

Clean Your House

This will be the first step in the entire process. Your home must be clean! If you are organized and everything in your home is pristine, this section may not be for you. Start by organizing your closets and pantries, vacuum floors, clean mirrors, dust, sweep, mop, and wipe down counter tops. Pick up your yard and put away any toys such as bicycles, sidewalk chalk, and miscellaneous items. Sweep porches, decks, and tidy up garages. Knowing kitchens and bathrooms are major selling points for homes, you will want to make sure those two areas are a main focus. Make your home look as clean as possible. Keep in mind that once your house is listed, you could have agents calling the day before or even the morning of a potential showing. Your home must remain show-worthy the majority of the time. A clean house is one that sells!

Personal Items

Remove all memorabilia or photographs. Take down any large artwork that may distract the prospective buyer from the appeal of your home. You want the buyer to fall in love with your property and imagine their belongings and life in the property as their next home. The more the prospective buyer can see themselves in your home the more likely they are to make an offer. This can also fall into the declutter category.

Pets

We all love our furry family members, but this could be a huge turn off for a prospective buyer that may be allergic to animals or maybe they don't like the thought of having a pet on the inside of the home. Some people associate pets with being unclean. No matter the reason, when a prospective buyer wants to view your home all proof of a pet, including water and food bowls, should be put away and the pet should be isolated to a designated area or should be completely removed from the home.

Staging

If you aren’t sure on how to accomplish the decluttered and organized look, hire a professional staging company to stage your home. These types of professionals have a way with emphasizing your home’s strengths while dampening its flaws. They can bring a fresh set of eyes to the situation and treat it as if they are a potential buyer. This can give you additional feedback on smaller things that you can change that you may not have otherwise thought about. It’s always a good thing to have a fresh set of eyes!

Valuables

Put anything of value in a safe or take it with you when your home is being shown to a potential buyer, especially if you are having an open house where multiple people may be viewing your home at one time. Open houses are targets for thieves. Your home is open to the public, not everyone will have an agent representing them and your agent may have multiple people talking to them at once so they could potentially get distracted. This can be a prime time for any sticky fingers to swipe anything of value. Guns, medication, family heirlooms, anything of value that can be put in a pocket or purse should be put away out of sight. Be aware that thieves may not steal at the open house or when viewing your home with an agent. They could be scoping out the inside of your home, learning the layout of your house, and making note of any valuables they see, so they can strike at a different date when they see that you aren't at home or a car isn't in your driveway. I'm not adding this section in the book to scare you in any way, but I am here to inform you that there is always a possibility of this happening and for you to be aware. Always protect yourself, your family, and your valuables.

Curb Appeal

Curb appeal is EVERYTHING! A potential buyers first glance of your house will set the tone for their entire experience. This glance will either be made by the listing pictures they see online or in person as they are physically driving by your property. Their opinion has been made within the first five seconds of seeing your home and you want to make that great first impression. Even if your home is not in a prime location, stepping up the curb appeal will make it more intriguing to the buyers and they may be less concerned about the location. Having a well-kept lawn, trimmed bushes, fresh mulch, etched out sidewalks, and planted flowers in flower beds or hanging baskets can be very pleasing to the eye. If your house tends to grow mildew, algae, or moss in the shade, power wash any areas that could be affected. These stains occur naturally over time. When house siding begins to turn green, it diminishes the exterior appearance of the home. Clean all leaves and debris from gutters. A fresh coat of paint on any shutters that may be faded will bring any house back to life and make your curb appeal pop!

Real Estate Agent

You want a real estate agent that is aggressive and just as eager to sell your home as you are. Do your homework! Do not hire an agent just because you see them on a billboard or on the table at your local restaurant. Ask around to friends and family. Word of mouth and how an agent has treated your friends and family speaks volumes about a person. Read reviews. Pay attention to local advertising, if an agent is on social media advertising for a home, they could be a great fit for you to sell your property fast. Online marketing allows agents to put your home in front of thousands of people in no time at all. The more people that see your home online will result in more showings. Newer agents are also ones to consider because they won't have as many listings so your home could be their main focus! Newer agents are learning techniques, marketing strategies, and can be just as aggressive as some of the agents that have been in the field for a while. Your house may be one of their only listings and if real estate is their only source of income, they will want your house sold yesterday. It is important to find a real estate agent that clicks well with you, that has your goals in mind, and that you feel comfortable going to if you have any questions or concerns. They need to be very approachable and knowledgeable. Agents, new or old, have one common goal, to work for you! They will hold your best interests in mind and negotiate for you. Selling your home is a huge decision and can sometimes become a complex transaction. You want to make sure you have the best representation that can negotiate on your behalf to successfully get you to the closing table.

For Sale by Owner

Selling your home yourself is always an option. Keep in mind that it is possible, but your home may sit longer on the market, because it may not get as much exposure as listing with a licensed real estate agent. Agents have access to the multiple listing service (MLS) that can advertise on hundreds of websites for you. They will also take care of the measurements and any pictures, advertising, disclosures, negotiating, paperwork, appraisals, and inspections. All of this can be very confusing to a person. Do your research and try to figure out which avenue is best for you.

Pictures

A picture is worth a thousand words! First impressions are made through the pictures you choose to advertise your property with. Make sure you take your pictures during the day when lighting is at its best. High quality pictures are going to make your property stand out when compared to other properties. Pictures need to portray the property as clean, spacious, and roomy. Hiring a professional photographer could be the difference in having your house on the market for a few days verses a few months. Pictures are also what drives the buyers through your door. This could be the single most important investment to simply get your property on someone's radar. If you choose to take the pictures yourself, make sure each room is clean and decluttered. You will want to stand in a corner to take the photo to make each room look its largest. In each bedroom, all beds should be made, clothing put away, and make sure all personal items are hidden. Try to include a window for bedrooms, if possible. Bathrooms should be cleaned with the toilet lid shut, and all personal toiletry items put away. Kitchens should be cleaned, sinks should be empty, large appliances wiped down, and all small kitchen appliances should be put away. Vacuum living areas and pick up any items on the floor. If you have pets, you will want to remove all pet items, including water/food bowls and liter boxes as discussed in the previous chapter.

3D Tours and Drone Aerial Shots

3D Tours is another type of marketing tool that allows potential buyers to view your property. A 3D Tour allows your potential buyers to virtually walk through the property without them having to leave the comfort of their current home. The tour will show the potential buyer the layout of the property and gives a basic walk-through starting at the front door. If you really want to standout with your marketing, you may want to consider this option.

Drones are great for homes with a large amount of land. If you have land that you want to display, this may be an option for you. Some drones have camera and video capability that can help highlight the property. Just an additional feature you may want to consider from a birds point of view.

Lighting

You want your home to be well lit at all times. Opening curtains for natural light to flow in can be really appealing to a prospective buyer. A dark or poorly lit home could come across as you are trying to hide flaws in your house. It can feel dark and depressing. You want prospective buyers to feel comfortable when inside your home and you want them to remember the natural lighting for a more cheery feel. Make sure all blown light bulbs are replaced and all corners are well lit. If showing your home after dark make sure all lighting works outside so all parties feel safe and secure. If a potential buyer doesn't feel safe, you can automatically mark them off of your possible buyer list. Nobody will buy a property if they feel uneasy or feel as if they could possibly be in danger. This can all be prevented from well lit areas.

Smells

When a buyer is scheduled to view your property make sure your house smells pleasant. There is nothing worse than entering a property and the first thing you smell is an animal, musty smells, or foul odor. Freshen up your home with Febreze to neutralize odors, maybe invest in a wax warmer, automatic mist spray, or if it's a nice day outside open some windows for fresh air. There are all sorts of ways to make the air smell fresh. Buyers will be turned off from your property if it smells bad!

Upgrades

Make small upgrades to your home to increase its value. Don't spend a ton of money on major remodels, because you may not get your money back. Focus on small upgrades where you will see a return on investment. Kitchens and bathrooms are the number one areas to focus on with seeing a return on your money. Everyone wants an updated kitchen and bathroom. Focus on smaller items such as hardware for the cabinets, upgrade your sink, or if you really feel adventurous upgrade to stainless steel appliances if you don't have them already. These could be huge selling points for your kitchen.

In your bathroom, focus on cabinet hardware, light fixtures, invest in a smaller cute vanity to spruce it up. Get a new shower curtain and hand towels to match to make your bathroom more pleasing to the eye. You don't have to replace a tub or rip up tile, these small upgrades can really make a large impact on the sell of your home!

Set Your Home Apart

Often times, agents show clients multiple listings in one evening. How do you want your home to be remembered? I always suggest having a few small bottles of water with either cookies or brownies left out for the buyers and include a note that says "Welcome, please take one." As mentioned before, always make your home look warm and inviting. This will help buyers remember your property because most people don't do this. They will always remember the house that was welcoming with wonderful goodies to eat.

Timing

Typically, Spring and Summer are the best times to sell your home. The weather has warmed up, people are out and about exploring the option to move. During the winter months, depending on your location, you may be competing against the weather with the cold and snow. There are also multiple holidays you have to work around with Thanksgiving, Christmas, and New Year's. People tend to not buy houses as much in November and December because of these factors. If you can hold off till the Spring to list your home, you should consider it. Tax season is in the spring time and some people use their tax refund as a down payment. When the weather warms up, you will see homes flying off the market. But be forewarned, that there will be increased inventory because most sellers list in the spring and summer months, so buyers can afford to be pickier.

Keep in mind that buyers in the winter months are usually people that NEED to buy. There are less houses on the market to choose from because most people wait until it's warm and pretty weather outside to list their homes. Less inventory on the market could be an advantage when selling.

Tough Skin

Selling your home isn't a walk in the park. It's work, a lot of hard work. You may be in a home that you have been in for over 30 years or maybe your home was a starter home and with a growing family you are looking to expand? No matter the reason, chances are, your home has sentimental value to you. You may think your home is perfect the way it stands or you may think it just needs a few cosmetic changes. Let me be the first to tell you, everyone has an opinion and opinions may hurt your feelings. Buyers will come into your home and rip it apart with their opinions and this home that you have lived in for "X" number of years that you think is perfect, will be tarnished with their opinions. Do NOT get your feelings hurt! Get tough skin! If they notice something that is outdated, chances are- it's outdated. If something is broken, let me be the first to tell you, a buyer will point it out. Take it for what it is and make the necessary changes. This is where a professional can help you weed through opinions and comments to make your home sell quickly. Real estate agents are there to help you through the process and make the transition smooth and easy, trust their opinions. They will negotiate on your behalf because they are there to help you. Don't take comments about your home personally- get tough skin!

Advertising

We live in an age where advertising can go from free to vastly expensive. Internet sites and apps such as Craigslist, Facebook, Instagram, Snapchat, Twitter and all forms of social media are free platforms to advertise your home. You can pay money to boost posts or have people advertise for you. Even if you have hired a real estate professional, do your part when it comes to your home. Send your active listing to family and friends and have them share your home on social media. Put up ads at your local grocery store. Send your listing to your homeowners' association email list and let your neighbors help advertise "who wants to be my neighbor?" You never know, they may have friends that are looking to move into your area.

Open House

Depending on your market, open houses may be a gem or a waste of time. If your market has houses listed for a day with multiple offers, you may not even get a chance to do an open house. In most areas, the market won’t be that strong so the possibility of an open house is more likely. When your agent schedules an open house don't get discouraged if only one or two potential buyers show up. Heck, nobody may show up! Don't get upset or discouraged. With today's digital society and 3D Tours. most people have already virtually walked through your home without even stepping foot on your property. A ton of people simply won't show up at an open house because of this. Some agents won't even do open houses anymore because they consider it a waste of time and money. If your agent mentions this, they are fully aware of how houses sell in their area and if they tell you this, it's not because they are lazy, they tell you this because it's true. If an open house is something you desire to have, just be honest with your agent. Agents want to make you happy, but most importantly they want to help you sell your home!

Ask for Feedback

After an open house or if a buyer views your property always ask for feedback. Ask what they liked about the property and about things they would change. Ask if they noticed anything that needs attention that you may have overlooked. It's always good to get a list of pros and cons so you can see what is working and what's not. Most of the time if you ask, buyers aren't shy they will tell you exactly what they thought. Be prepared to get an honest opinion and make changes, if necessary.

Home Health Inspection

Several companies will offer a home health inspection. This inspection is *free* and it could be helpful in selling your property fast. You can include a copy of this form and make it available at showings or open houses. It will also make you aware if there are any damages that you did not previously know about. It's better to find it and fix it before it's put on the market and before the buyer's inspection finds it. If that happens often times it gives buyers leverage on lowering the price or making a list of fixes that must be complete before the final walk through. Knowledge is power and if you can make an easy fix, I'd recommend doing it.

Loan Programs

Some loan programs have more restrictions than others. Potential buyers may be limited on making an offer depending on which type of loan they are approved for. If you see peeling paint in your home, if your electrical outlets are outdated, or if you have stairs with no hand railings you may want to consider updating or adding those items before listing. By not doing those simple updates, you could be excluding a group of buyers whose loan program requires those updates to be made.

Closing Costs

Be aware that some buyers may ask the seller to pay for closing costs or any prepaid items. These are fees and charges that are associated with purchasing a home. Closing costs are fees associated with the loan, lender's fees, title company's fees, appraisal fees, etc. Prepaid items are items that have to be paid prior to closing, an example of this could be the first year home owners insurance premium or the initial escrow deposit. Just be aware that you could potentially be asked to pay for these costs and that it could be deducted from the proceeds of the sale of your home.

Pricing

Pricing determines who looks at your property. If you over price your home, it will sit on the market and simply won’t sell. If you under price your home, you are selling yourself short out of the money you could have pocketed. How do you know the correct price to list your home at to obtain your maximum money without giving it away or without it sitting on the market for ages? This is where it is beneficial to hire a real estate agent. They can run a comparative market analysis on homes that have recently sold with the same amount of bedrooms, bathrooms, and square footage in the same location and can also compare homes that are currently on the market. This will allow you to make an informed and educated decision on what price you should list your home for. We often see Zillow's Zestimate and want to list our house for that amount. Zillow doesn't take into consideration if a house has been updated, if it's outdated, or any changes a homeowner may have made. The Zestimate doesn't consider location or any comparative properties. Don't be fooled by the number on the screen, because it's not always correct. Be informed and be realistic!

My Wish for You

I hope this book helps you make educated and informed decisions when listing your home. I want you to get the best bang for your buck and I want you to do it in record time. I am a firm believer in moving fast and doing it right the first time. Knowledge is power and empowerment is the tool to be successful. I wish you the best and happy selling!

Lightning Source UK Ltd.
Milton Keynes UK
UKHW011436010219
336574UK00009B/450/P

9 780368 183140